First World War
and Army of Occupation
War Diary
France, Belgium and Germany

58 DIVISION
Headquarters, Branches and Services
Royal Army Veterinary Corps
Deputy Assistant Director Veterinary Services
5 September 1915 - 25 February 1916

WO95/2994/5

The Naval & Military Press Ltd
www.nmarchive.com
Published in association with The National Archives

Published by

The Naval & Military Press Ltd

Unit 10 Ridgewood Industrial Park,

Uckfield, East Sussex,

TN22 5QE England

Tel: +44 (0) 1825 749494

www.naval-military-press.com

www.nmarchive.com

This diary has been reprinted in facsimile from the original. Any imperfections are inevitably reproduced and the quality may fall short of modern type and cartographic standards.

© **Crown Copyright**
Images reproduced by permission of The National Archives, London, England, 2015.

Contents

Document type	Place/Title	Date From	Date To
Heading	WO95/2994/5		
Heading	58 Division (2/1 London Div) ADVS 1915 Sep-1916 Feb		
Miscellaneous	The Statement	02/09/1915	02/09/1915
Miscellaneous	Veterinary Services		
War Diary	Ipswich	05/09/1915	22/01/1916
War Diary	Needham-Market	04/02/1916	25/02/1916

WO 95/2994/5

58 DIVISION
(2/1 LONDON DIV)

A.D.V.S

1915 SEP — 1916 FEB

"THE STATEMENT"

ACCOMPANYING THE WAR DIARY.

OF

LIEUT. COLONEL. H.M. MAXWELL.

A.D. OF V.S.
58th. (LONDON) DIVISION.

IPSWICH.

2nd. SEPTEMBER. 1915.

6666666666666666666666666666666666666666666666

VETERINARY SERVICES.

UNIT. Army Veterinary Corps.

DIVISION 58th. (London) Division.

MOBILIZATION CENTRE. London.

TEMPORARY WAR STATION. Bisley.

Stations since occupied subsequent to

CONCENTRATION Crowborough and Ipswich.

TRAINING. The training of the Veterinary Section of the 69th.
East Anglian Division at Bury St Edmunds (Administered by this Division) is proceeding very satisfactory under Captain A.R. Routledge, A.V.C. (T).

During the month orders were received to form a Mobile Veterinary Section for service overseas, This has been done, and the Section is now complete as regards personnel

VETERINARY SERVICES.

There has been but slight sickness during the month. Skin diseases continue to occur, although cases have been largely reduced by regular and thorough inspections, and the periodical treatment of all horses both affected and healthy.

Forage Generally fair, but several lots of hay have been condemned.

Forges and tools continue short although there have been repeated promises of deficiencies being made good.

Disinfection. of horse rugs and stable gear is carried out as considered necessary.

Cast Horses. A fair number of remounts have been supplied to the Division during the month, and old and unserviceable horses have been cast.

Transport Services. Satisfactory.

Remount Supply. Several hundreds of remounts have been received by this Division during the month, but some of these have only been fit for casting being over 15 years old and worn out.

DISCIPLINE. Very good.

ADMINISTRATIVE. Good.

MEDICIAL SERVICES. Good.

SUPPLY SERVICES. Good.

Billeting and Hutting The men are billeted, and all arrangements are satisfactory.

CHANNEL OF CORRESPONDENCE IN ROUTINE MATTERS.

Divisional Headquarters, and Brigade Commanders.

PREPARING OF UNITS FOR IMPERIAL SERVICE.

The men of the Veterinary Section receive regular instructions in the duties of Collecting Parties, and in riding.

6666666666666666666666

H. M. Maxwell
Lieut. Colonel,
A.D.V.S.
58th (London) Division.

Army Form C. 2118

WAR DIARY
or
INTELLIGENCE SUMMARY
(Erase heading not required.)

Instructions regarding War Diaries and Intelligence Summaries are contained in F.S. Regs., Part II. and the Staff Manual respectively. Title Pages will be prepared in manuscript.

58th (LONDON) DIVISION.
A.D.V.S.
Lieut. Colonel,

1 - OCT. 1915

Place	Date	Hour	Summary of Events and Information	Remarks and references to Appendices
IPSWICH.	5/9/15	11.am.	A.D.V.S. inspected the Remounts of the Divisional Artillery at Ipswich.	
do	9/9/15	3.30.pm.	A.D.V.S. inspected the 1/2nd. London Brigade. R.F.A. at Saxmundham.	
do	10/9/15	11.30.am.	A.D.V.S. inspected the Divisional Veterinary Hospital at Bury St. Edmunds.	
do	11/9/15	10.30.am.	A.D.V.S. inspected the 1/3rd. London Brigade, R.F.A. at Framlingham.	
do	11/9/15	12.noon.	A.D.V.S. inspected the 1/2nd. London Brigade, R.F.A. at Saxmundham.	
do	11/9/15	3.pm.	A.D.V.S. inspected the 1/1st. London Brigade. R.F.A. at Warren Heath.	
do	11/9/15	4.pm.	A.D.V.S. inspected the 1/4th. London (How) Brigade R.F.A. at Warren Heath.	
do	11/9/15	4.30.pm.	A.D.V.S. inspected the 1/1st. London R.G.A., at Warren Heath.	
do	12/9/15	3.30.pm.	A.D.V.S. inspected the Divisional R.E. at Wickham Market.	
do	19/9/15	11.am.	A.D.V.S. inspected the 1/4th. London (How) Brigade. R.F.A. at Warren Heath.	
do	19/9/15	12.am.	A.D.V.S. inspected the 1/1st. London Brigade. R.F.A. Warren Heath.	
do	21/9/15	3.30.pm.	A.D.V.S. inspected the 1/3rd. London Brigade. R.F.A. at Framlingham.	
do	22/9/15	3.30.pm.	A.D.V.S. inspected the 1/2nd. London Brigade. R.F.A. at Saxmundham.	
do	30/9/15	12.15.	A.D.V.S. inspected the 173rd. Infantry Brigade with A.D.V.S. 1st. Army, at Ipswich.	
do	30/9/15	3.pm.	A.D.V.S. inspected the 175th. Infantry Brigade, with A.D.V.S.1st. Army, at Woodbridge,	
do	30/9/15	3.30.pm.	A.D.V.S. inspected the 2/3rd.Field Ambulance at Woodbridge with A.D.V.S. 1st. Army,	

Army Form C. 2118

WAR DIARY
or
INTELLIGENCE SUMMARY

(Erase heading not required.)

OCTOBER, 1915.

N I L

Ipswich.
2nd. November. 1915.

[Signature]
Lieut. Colonel.
A.D.V.S.
58th (London) Division.

Place	Date	Hour	Summary of Events and Information	Remarks and references to Appendices

Instructions regarding War Diaries and Intelligence Summaries are contained in F. S. Regs., Part II. and the Staff Manual respectively. Title Pages will be prepared in manuscript.

1875 Wt. W593/826 1,000,000 4/15 J.B.C. & A. A.D.S.S./Forms/C. 2118.

Army Form C. 2118

WAR DIARY
or
INTELLIGENCE SUMMARY
(Erase heading not required.)

Instructions regarding War Diaries and Intelligence Summaries are contained in F. S. Regs., Part II. and the Staff Manual respectively. Title Pages will be prepared in manuscript.

Place	Date	Hour	Summary of Events and Information	Remarks and references to Appendices
	21st. November. 1915.		Mobile Veterinary Section joined this Division from Tunbridge Wells.	
Ipswich.	3rd. December. 1915.			

E.M. Maxwell
Lieut. Col.
A.D.V.S.
58th. (London) Division.

1875 Wt. W593/826 1,000,000 4/15 J.B.C. & A. A.D.S.S./Forms/C. 2118.

Army Form C. 2118

WAR DIARY
or
INTELLIGENCE SUMMARY

(Erase heading not required.)

Instructions regarding War Diaries and Intelligence Summaries are contained in F.S. Regs., Part II. and the Staff Manual respectively. Title Pages will be prepared in manuscript.

Place	Date	Hour	Summary of Events and Information	Remarks and references to Appendices
Ipswich.	22nd. Dec.		Major Hobson A.V.C. granted one month sick leave from the 22nd. December. 1915.	
do	31st. Dec.		Captain H. Anthony, A.V.C.(T) took over charge of the 58th. Mobile Veterinary Section.	
			Ipswich.	
			4th. January. 1916.	

[Stamp: 58th (LONDON) DIVISION 4 - JAN 1916]

W.M. Maxwell
Lieut. Colonel,
A.D.V.S.
58th (LONDON) DIVISION.

1875 Wt. W593/826 1,000,000 4/15 J.B.C. & A. A.D.S.S./Forms/C. 2118.

Army Form C. 2118

WAR DIARY

or

~~INTELLIGENCE SUMMARY~~

A.D.V.S. 58th. (London) DIVISION.
Redhouse Park, Ipswich.

(Erase heading not required.)

Instructions regarding War Diaries and Intelligence Summaries are contained in F. S. Regs., Part II. and the Staff Manual respectively. Title Pages will be prepared in manuscript.

Place	Date	Hour	Summary of Events and Information	Remarks and references to Appendices
Ipswich.	22nd. January, 1916.		Captain William Awde, A.V.C.(T) took over A.D.V.S. duties from Lt. Colonel. H.M. Maxwell, *WA*	
			Ipswich. 1st. February. 1916.	
			William Awde Captain, A.D.V.S. 58th. (London) Division.	

[Stamp: 58th (LONDON) DIVISION * GENERAL STAFF * 1 - FEB. 1916]

Army Form C. 2118

WAR DIARY
or
INTELLIGENCE SUMMARY

(Erase heading not required.)

H.Q. 58th (London) Divisional R.E.

Instructions regarding War Diaries and Intelligence Summaries are contained in F.S. Regs., Part II. and the Staff Manual respectively. Title Pages will be prepared in manuscript.

Place	Date	Hour	Summary of Events and Information	Remarks and references to Appendices
NEEDHAM MARKET	4/2/16	10.0 A.M.	Brigadier-Genl A.G. Paper B.B, R.E. (Inspector of R.E.) inspected 2/1st & 2/2nd & 1/5th London Field Coys.	
" "	19/2/16	10.0 A.M.	Brigadier-Genl C.J. Bogges BB, M.B.O, D.S.O. G.O.C. 58th Division, inspected the 2/1st & 2/2nd London Field Coys.	
" "	21/2/16	2.50 A.M. 10 9.45 A.M.	The 2/1st & 2/2nd London Field Coys. left this Station to proceed Overseas	
" "	22/2/16	11.45 p.m.	The 2/1st Wessex Field Coy arrived	
" "	23/2/16	2.30 A.M.	The 2/2nd Wessex Field Coy arrived	
" "	25/2/16	10.4 A.M.	The details of 2/1st & 2/2nd London Field Coys left this Station to join 3rd Line at Esher	

Geo. W. Walkers
Lt. Col. R.E. (TF)
C.R.E. 58th (London) Division

3/3/16

Army Form C. 2118

WAR DIARY

INTELLIGENCE/SUMMARY

(Erase heading not required.)

A.D.V.S.
58th. (London) Division.

Place	Date	Hour	Summary of Events and Information	Remarks and references to Appendices
Red House Park, Ipswich, March 3rd. 1916.	February, 1916.		N I L	

Instructions regarding War Diaries and Intelligence Summaries are contained in F. S. Regs., Part II. and the Staff Manual respectively. Title Pages will be prepared in manuscript.

[Stamp: 58th (LONDON) DIVISION — 5 MAR 1916 — GENERAL]

........William Ansth........ Major,
A.D.V.S.
58th. (London) Division.

1875 Wt. W593/826 1,000,000 4/15 J.B.C. & A. A.D.S.S./Forms/C. 2118.

www.ingramcontent.com/pod-product-compliance
Lightning Source LLC
Chambersburg PA
CBHW081515160426
43193CB00014B/2700